ARNIM WINKLER

GIOTTO

TRANSLATED FROM THE GERMAN BY
ANNE ROSS

THE UFFICI PRESS S.A.
MILANO

Front Cover Illustration:

THE RAISING OF LAZARUS. (Detail)
Scrovegni Chapel, Padua, Italy.

Back Cover Illustration:

THE SAINT APPEARS TO THE BISHOP OF ASSISI
AND TO THE MONK AUGUSTINE. (Detail)
Bardi Chapel, Church of Santa Croce, Florence, Italy.

GIOTTO

A study of Giotto (1266 - 1337) can best begin with a comparison drawn from our times, by imagining an artist bound to and conditioned by his own era, whose paintings can be appreciated quickly — perhaps even *too* quickly — and who yet arouses a storm of protest over his " impossible pictures ".

Such pictures, say contemporaries, by tacit consent is not painting, because they correspond in no way with what one can see to-day or knows from the past. They are, in fact, unacceptable. This point of view owes nothing to logical reasoning but it a wholly emotional reaction. The angry arguments range from protests against sacrilege to claims that his paintings insult those who look at them. It follows logically that the innovator also finds partisans, who will defend him out of contrariness or conviction, or perhaps just because he stands in opposition to precedent.

Such a contemporary example can provide the starting-point for a study of Giotto, by helping to bridge the gap of more than six hundred years which divides his age from ours, and also by giving the reader a deeper understanding of the events which took place within a narrow, and quite different, setting in the first years of the fourteenth century.

This different setting was medieval Italy long before the rise and magnificence of the Renaissance City States, when it was still a fragmented society, which since the fall of the Roman Empire had found its basis, not in any general or national order, but only in the one principle which had emerged from the rubble — the Christian faith and its mystical observance. The fount of cultural strength — as we might describe it to-day — sprang exclusively from the church, and later also from the cloister, and in these the people found their refuge in tradition and their help in the often comfortless present.

The narrower their lives and the greater their fear, the stronger became the forms in which supernatural aid appeared to support them. Whether in liturgy or other forms of worship, or in the pictorial portrayals of the scriptures and of Christ the Redeemer made for the simple illiterate people, the existing forms had to be maintained. At such times men are like children, who cannot bear a single word to be altered in an oft-repeated story or legend, but demand an established, integral text.

Naturally the conception of art, as we use the word to-day, consisted solely of ecclesiastical illustrations, or more precisely, of illuminations in a hand-written passage of scripture, which became the visible portrayal of the church as the place where one most easily finds grace. This symbolism demanded a form capable of portraying God's high, unearthly greatness, and of making eternity recognizable, together with an impressive magnificence, and a monumental conception which could intensify and exalt belief.

Byzantine art derived its characteristics from these requirements, and from the fourth century on its triumphal progress spread throughout all the western world, following in the wake of political influence and military conquest, extending its realm over the whole of Italy and under Otto II into Germany too.

Its greatest triumphs were in architecture, in frescoes, and even more in richly coloured mosaics, which often took the place of painting at that time because they gave the artist greater scope for expression and a stronger range of colours, and promised to last longer. In Byzantine art man is not a part of his environment, but stands detached from a golden or coloured background, which embraces him like a curtain to shut out the "beyond", and sets him off like a rock against which lap the waves of time. Byzantine figures are as realistic

4

CRUCIFIX IN
SANTA MARIA
NOVELLA,
Florence

ST. DAMIAN'S
CRUCIFIX
SPEAKS TO
ST. FRANCIS
(Detail)
Assisi

THE ECSTASY OF ST. FRANCIS. ASSISI

THE TRIAL BY FIRE BEFORE THE SULTAN
(Detail: The Sultan's Priests). 1296-97. Church of St. Francis, Assisi

as portraits, though far from representing any single individual, each one seems to portray a type, as though everyone destined by appearance for a certain rôle in life were rolled into one and distilled into the portrait of an ideal. Hence the almost total lack of movement, for even the stance of the figures is stylized and they look us straight and hard in the eyes. When the apostles look at Our Lord, or Christ turns towards the adulteress, their bodies hardly seem affected. In most cases only the eyes are directed towards the object of their regard, and sometimes the head is inclined without the position of the body following it. At the very most a three-quarter face is shown and one has to look closely to detect even that. Thus the church's graphic world became an ordered realm of salvation, expressed in a set pictorial language which to the spectator conveyed and emanated comfort and peace.

Into this tranquil and orderly world Giotto now stepped, with his portrayals of individual personalities. He created no apostle-type, who in spite of seeming like a portrait could well have been the sum of every possible model for that apostle, but a definite, completely individual character, who by chance at that moment was best suited by his personal appearance to fill a rôle in that particular scriptural story. To capture the inner being, character, bearing, actions — everything, in fact, which the rôle required — through the medium of a person who looked as though he had lived in Biblical times, was the task Giotto set himself.

In a period characterized by the search for absolute holiness, he began to introduce a human element into the lives of the saints, as though he was saying: "If the story had taken place yesterday, this is how it would have looked". He meant no disrespect nor sacrilege by this, but rather a deeper, more intense participation, as though seeing these great events before his very eyes and therefore feeling their impact all the more strongly.

Individuals act individually, making their own mark on the world, and this can be conveyed most clearly by painting them in profils, while hand gestures give clarity and point to characters. As the previous Byzantine paintings had used the full-face view to depict a type, so the profile view is suitable for clarifying

THE APPARITION OF THE FIERY CHARIOT. (Detail)
Upper Church of St. Francis, Assisi

the new element of personal feeling in the characters portrayed. The unusual position of a head turned to one side so compels the attention that one can almost tell what the person is saying. The event portrayed in the picture emerges like a narrative from the movement of the characters. The spectator immediately knows from his own experience what the character is feeling, reading it, so to speak, from the picture.

Giotto's novel visual approach was of course not to be regarded as an original discovery to challenge the existing world. Only those who were fast rooted in tradition saw it as such, and greeted it with angry protests. In fact this change of vision was inevitable in the historical context, since men were turning away from too great a formalism in thought, and change was already in the air. By virtue of his genius Giotto was the one who sensed this change in the spiritual atmosphere and was in a position to express it. His new approach, therefore, most strongly influenced the more aware spirits, who then became his supporters and patrons. A middle group found themselves torn between the two positions and only after a time felt their way towards the new mode of painting. Giotto therefore found himself caught in a clash of conflicting opinions.

The comparison with a modern artist helps one to grasp the varied reactions and the range of widely differing view-points, without taking it as applicable only to the work of a genius like Giotto. The point which distinguishes this as the case of a genius is that his way sooner or later prevailed, and became the only accepted form.

The opposition to Giotto has not survived in any valid form down to modern times; of the struggles over his work the only evidence remaining to-day are the incomprehensible eulogies which, wildly overstating the case, have gone down in the descriptions, of contemporary authors as retrospective accounts of the protagonists opinions. They call Giotto a "natural painter", which is clearly untrue, because even he always stylized nature, but his method of portrayal seemed to his contemporaries excessively naturalistic compared with that of his predecessors. A similar analogy lay behind Boccaccio's statement that all pre-Giotto art was dead

St. Francis Drives
the Devils Out
of Arezzo. (Detail)
Church
of St. Francis,
Assisi

ST. FRANCIS REVERED BY A SIMPLE MAN
1296-97. Upper Church of St. Francis, Assisi, Italy

ST. FRANCIS GIVES AWAY HIS CLOAK. 1296-97. Upper Church of St. Francis, Assisi

ST. FRANCIS APPEARS TO POPE GREGORY IX (Detail)
Upper Church of St. Francis, Assisi, Italy

ST. FRANCIS PREACHING BEFORE POPE HONORIUS III. 1298-1300
Upper Church of St. Francis, Assisi, Italy

and buried. This is obviously out of the question, and we to-day see no reason to condemn Byzantine art, even if we feel greater interest in the artistic revolution started by Giotto.

* * *

One of these later enthusiastic supporters of Giotto was the Italian sculptor and goldsmith Lorenzo Ghilberti, who published in his memoirs an account of the careers of the Tuscan painters after Giotto. The following story of his is often quoted:

"The art of painting started its revival in Etruria, in a small hamlet called Vespignano, not far from Florence, where was born a child with a wonderful talent, who could draw a sheep to the life. One day the painter Cimabue, on his way to Bologna, passed through the hamlet, and saw the child sitting on the ground, drawing a sheep on a slate. He marvelled to see a boy at this tender age drawing so well and, recognizing that he possessed a natural gift asked his name. The child answered: "My name is Giotto; my father is called Bondone and lives in this house". Cimabue, a man held in great esteem, took the boy to his father, who was very poor, and asked to be given the child. The father agreed, Cimabue took Giotto away with him and thus it came about that he became Cimabue's pupil".

In 1276, the year he left Colle di Vespignano for Florence, he was ten years old, and Cimabue was thirty-six.

"Now the boy began regular lessons in art, in which he made such quick progress that he soon left his master far behind".

Some early works in the chapel behind the high altar in the Abbey Church in Florence have disappeared, but a very large crucifix in the church of Santa Maria Novella (see page 5) has survived. Then followed twenty-eight powerful life-size narrative paintings from the legends of St. Francis, which Giotto painted in the Upper Church of St. Francis in Assisi in 1296 and 1297, and which presented to his contemporaries his remarkable new form of figure-painting.

ST. FRANCIS GIVES
AWAY HIS CLOAK
(Detail)
Upper Church of
St. Francis,
Assisi, Italy

Among all the orders — Carthusian, Cistercian, Premonstratensian, Dominican, Carmelite, and Augustinian — founded between 1086 and 1244, the Franciscans, founded by St. Francis of Assisi (1181 - 1226), had the greatest effect on the people of the time. Here at last was someone who looked down from above on those who lived in misery and need — the son of a very rich cloth-merchant dedicating himself after a youth spent in knightly pursuits, to voluntary poverty and charity. He attracted disciples, founded the new, socialistic type of begging order and thereby became the beloved friend of the poor and the dispossessed. Seventy years after the saint's death his deeds had already turned into a living, powerful legend, which demanded an effective narrative expression, and Giotto was the ideal painter to illustrate it, which he did in a new and deeply moving way.

Examples of St. Francis's contacts with simple people can be seen on pages 13, 14 and 18; his vocation to the service of God on pages 6 and 7. His adventurous journey in 1219 to the Sultan Al Kamil, who he wished to convert, is represented by the pictures of the ordeal by fire, a miracle performed before the Sultan, while his priests look on in sullen rage, (pages 3 and 41, the latter a later picture from the legend of St. Francis, which was to captivate Giotto throughout his life).

Personal difficulties, especially due to the too harsh rules of the order, caused the saint to withdraw to the solitude of Mount Alvernia outside Arezzo, where he performed miracles (page 12). In 1223 Gregory IX gave the order its definitive and milder rules which were revealed to him in a vision (page 15), thus making a compromise with the strict Franciscan way of thought, which could be traced back to St. Gioacchino da Fiore (1130 - 1202) who in 1190 founded a very severe monastic order. His story therefore became a part of the Franciscan legend (pages 21 and 22). In 1224 St. Francis became the first historically documented case of stigmatization, and on 3rd October, 1226, he died. A painting of the saint was already to be found in 1228 in a church in Subiaco, but Giotto's work in Assisi in 1296 and 1297 and in Florence after 1317 established him as the first great and inspiring illustrator of the legend.

ISAAC BANISHES
ESAU (Detail)
Upper Church of
St. Francis,
Assisi, Italy

ST. GIOACCHINO'S
DREAM (Detail)
Scrovegni Chapel,
Padua, Italy

ST. GIOACCHINO WITH HIS FLOCK. Scrovegni Chapel, Padua, Italy

THE ANNUNCIATION
(Detail: The
Virgin Mary)
Scrovegni Chapel,
Padua, Italy

THE PRESENTATION OF JESUS IN THE TEMPLE. Scrovegni Chapel, Padua, Italy

THE ACADEMY
MADONNA
(Detail from the
reproduction
on page 43)

St. John the Evangelist
Jacquemart-André
Museum, Châlis,
near d'Ermenonville,
(Oise), France

34

St. Lawrence
Jacquemart-André
Museum, Châlis,
near d'Ermenonville,
(Oise), France

placed them. Their new, monumental and plastically treated figures give them an unsurpassed dramatic effect, which in turn provides Giotto's narratives with a hitherto unknown illustrative force.

This effect was reinforced by a unified use of light and by attempts at a sense of perspective, which also contributed to the dense, self-contained character of Giotto's pictorial realm. Apart from all these innovations which pointed towards the future, and which Giotto introduced with magnificent verve, his works naturally contain many of the hallmarks of a medieval painter. In spite of all his individualizing, his figures constantly tend towards standardization, admittedly in quite a different form from that of Byzantine art, yet strong enough from a modern standpoint to arouse opposition to the contemporary view of him as a naturalistic painter. To this should be added the imprint of a certain craftsmanship in his works which gave them their characteristic style and made it possible for others — pupils, assistants, successors — to emulate him. This is the reason why a school could be founded on the principles of Giotto's artistic revolution: it was imitable, and in fact the whole fourteenth century bore the stamp of his style.

Only once the direct effect of Giotto's work had exhausted itself could early Renaissance painting again depend on the artist's own vision, and the striving towards the interpretation of reality attain its dazzling peaks. Also here Giotto was the great impetus, the creator of something fundamentally new, who led the artistic transition from the middle ages into a new era.

THE FLIGHT INTO EGYPT. Scrovegni Chapel, Padua, Italy

THE WORSHIP OF
THE THREE KINGS
(Detail)
Scrovegni Chapel,
Padua, Italy

THE WORSHIP OF
THE THREE KINGS
(Detail)
Scrovegni Chapel,
Padua, Italy

THE BETRAYAL OF JESUS. Scrovegni Chapel, Padua, Italy

THE ACADEMY
MADONNA
(Detail from the
reproduction
on page 43)

34

St. Lawrence
Jacquemart-André
Museum, Châlis,
near d'Ermenonville,
(Oise), France

placed them. Their new, monumental and plastically treated figures give them an unsurpassed dramatic effect, which in turn provides Giotto's narratives with a hitherto unknown illustrative force.

This effect was reinforced by a unified use of light and by attempts at a sense of perspective, which also contributed to the dense, self-contained character of Giotto's pictorial realm. Apart from all these innovations which pointed towards the future, and which Giotto introduced with magnificent verve, his works naturally contain many of the hallmarks of a medieval painter. In spite of all his individualizing, his figures constantly tend towards standardization, admittedly in quite a different form from that of Byzantine art, yet strong enough from a modern standpoint to arouse opposition to the contemporary view of him as a naturalistic painter. To this should be added the imprint of a certain craftsmanship in his works which gave them their characteristic style and made it possible for others — pupils, assistants, successors — to emulate him. This is the reason why a school could be founded on the principles of Giotto's artistic revolution: it was imitable, and in fact the whole fourteenth century bore the stamp of his style.

Only once the direct effect of Giotto's work had exhausted itself could early Renaissance painting again depend on the artist's own vision, and the striving towards the interpretation of reality attain its dazzling peaks. Also here Giotto was the great impetus, the creator of something fundamentally new, who led the artistic transition from the middle ages into a new era.

THE DEPOSITION. 1304-1305. Scrovegni Chapel, Padua, Italy

THE LAST
JUDGMENT
(Detail from
Hell). 1304
Scrovegni
Chapel,
Padua, Italy

39

The
Resurrection
(Detail)
Scrovegni
Chapel,
Padua, Italy

FROM THE LIFE
OF ST. FRANCIS
(Detail from the
Trial by Fire
before the Sultan)
after 1317
Bardi Chapel,
Church of
Santa Croce,
Florence, Italy

ST. STEPHEN
c. 1320-1330
Horne Foundation,
Florence, Italy

ACADEMY MADONNA
Uffizi Gallery,
Florence, Italy

43

BUSTE OF AN ANGEL. Mosaic of the « Navicella ». The Vatican

BUST OF AN ANGEL. Mosaic Medallion from St. Peter's Church, The Vatican, Rome. 1298-1300

ILLUSTRATIONS

In the same presentation:

RENOIR   PICASSO
VAN GOGH   REMBRANDT
LAUTREC   EL GRECO
GOYA   GAUGUIN
GIOTTO   CÉZANNE
          DEGAS
          DELACROIX
          CRANACH
          MANET

In preparation:

BRUEGHEL
MONET